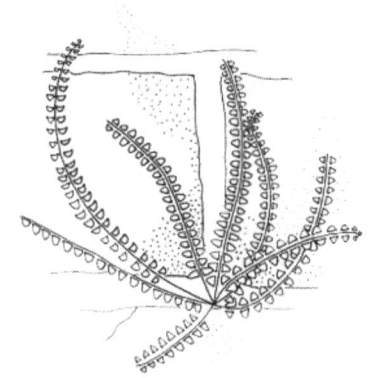

There You Are

A COLLECTION OF HAND LETTERED POEMS ABOUT MOTHERHOOD

Copyright Elisabeth Pike 2017.

All rights reserved. No part of this book may be reproduced in any form without written permission from the publisher.

Published by Little Bird Editions.

There You Are

How Terrifying
SNOW
Afterwards
Darkness
There You Are
LOVE POEM
~~Scan~~
Laundry
~~Something in between~~
Pied Piper
A Walk Near Shere
WAITING FOR IVY
Lemon Cake
~~Moment~~
Guildford
Crying in public places
MY BOY, MY GIRL
Spring Nights
DECEMBER
Charterhouse
Little Park
Trembling Heart
Type One
Thunderstorm
Half-past Nine
The Bells
KIND
Kiss on the lips
LITTLE CAR
Five-thirty
Sand Martins
~~Inwood~~
UNCOUPLING

Raye

How terrifying
that night we first brought you
home!
I did not trust your lungs
to work by themselves
And I reached over in the dark to you,
to feel for your nose and lips,
to make sure you weren't smothered.
You would snuffle and
grunt and I would move my
hand
and lie there in the pitch dark,
my body turned to you,
guardian,
watcher of your little soul.
I chased away my sleep with
worry as I listened for your breaths,
feeling like the only
one in the world
who could hear you, who was
listening out for you.

We were at a friends' house
　　the night before and opened
the door to the flurry of snowflakes.
WE DROVE HOME SLOWLY WITH THE WINDOWS OPEN;
IT WAS COLD, AND THE SNOW FELL IN SPIRALS.

It was unlike anything we'd seen,
even then, and in the morning,
we woke, breath-held to see it —
white and deep, like a dream.
THE PHONE-CALL CAME SAYING THAT THE SCHOOL
WHERE WE WORKED WAS CLOSED AND WE GOT DRESSED
AND RAN OUT IN THE STREET. It was so quiet
that it seemed no-one else had even
woken. WE WERE AS EXCITED AS SCHOOL CHILDREN, RUNNING
TO JEN'S AT EIGHT IN THE MORNING BECAUSE WE DIDN'T KNOW
WHAT ELSE TO DO. We walked around the
streets, took a tray up to the Downs
and made tracks in it. funny to
think that that's where you began,
out of joy you were sown, little bird,
settling under the snow.

In the darkness of night, I lie between the two of you and check that I can single you out.

One by one your breaths fall like stars in the dark.

THERE YOU ARE

little pulse of life.
Your slow breaths come crackling through
on the monitor.
I LIFT IT TO MY EAR EVERY NOW AND THEN
AND HEAR THE STATIC
AND PRESS IT CLOSER TO
HEAR YOU THERE.
I think of the first scan we had,
when we saw you
wriggling away;
your spine a
LIT UP FISH
YOU HAD SO MUCH ROOM THEN,
SO MUCH ENERGY,
AND SWAM AROUND,
unaware that we were watching,
already delighting in you.

LOVE POEM

I love him in the bath tonight. He is sitting in front of me, and his shoulder blades jut out like little wings beneath his pale skin. I'm humbled with it all again, which I haven't felt in so long; the tears and tiredness having got in the way. BUT here it is again, the flash of wonder at being just you, YOU ♡ for having grown in me, all by yourself, for knowing when to be born, for being here now, all smiles and squawks. I run my finger down your soapy back and remember how it looked on the scan, little fish.

AND I remember that I fell in love with your father for the silly things like that: his shoulder blades, the shape of his toes, the sound of his laugh.

the lady in THE ULTRASOUND ROOM SAYS 'oh look at its little feet, its being very well behaved,' AND I THINK THIS IS SOMEONE WHO IS JUST doing her job and yet she acts as if I am important. HERE SHE IS, BABY, A LOVING MY perfect stranger to her.

AND THERE YOU ARE. ITS ASTOUNDING HOW ALIVE, HOW AT HOME YOU ARE. like nothing we know, nothing we can remember.

ELEVEN MONTH OLD SAM LAUGHS AS I LIE ON THE BENCH WITH MY TUMMY OUT. HE DOESN'T UNDERSTAND WHEN WE TELL HIM THAT THERE IS HIS BABY SISTER THERE ON THE SCREEN.

HE JUST LAUGHS AT THE BOX OF BLUE RUBBER GLOVES, HIS FACE IN THE MIRROR, THE LIGHTS IN THE CEILING, WONDERING AT THINGS ALL THE WHILE.

Laundry

I stand out amongst the whites in the yard, (still hung up to dry though it is getting dark.) I gather them in, the stone slabs rough and warm beneath my feet.

A hundred voices hum and a few doors slam at the close of day in this town. Yellow kitchen light spills across the car park where the boys from up the road do tricks on their skateboards. The scrape of their wheels on the tarmac etches itself into my remembering.

Flotsam nudges up to each back door, leaving unwanted tidelines. Things heard around here cannot be unheard. Everyone knows what goes on, but still, when they wake, in the cold morning light, they prowl around the edges of their property, guarding their lives, their small secrets.

And I mine, I suppose, for behind this blue gate, and beyond this tatty yard, within this see-through house, as frail as a skeleton are all my life's treasures.

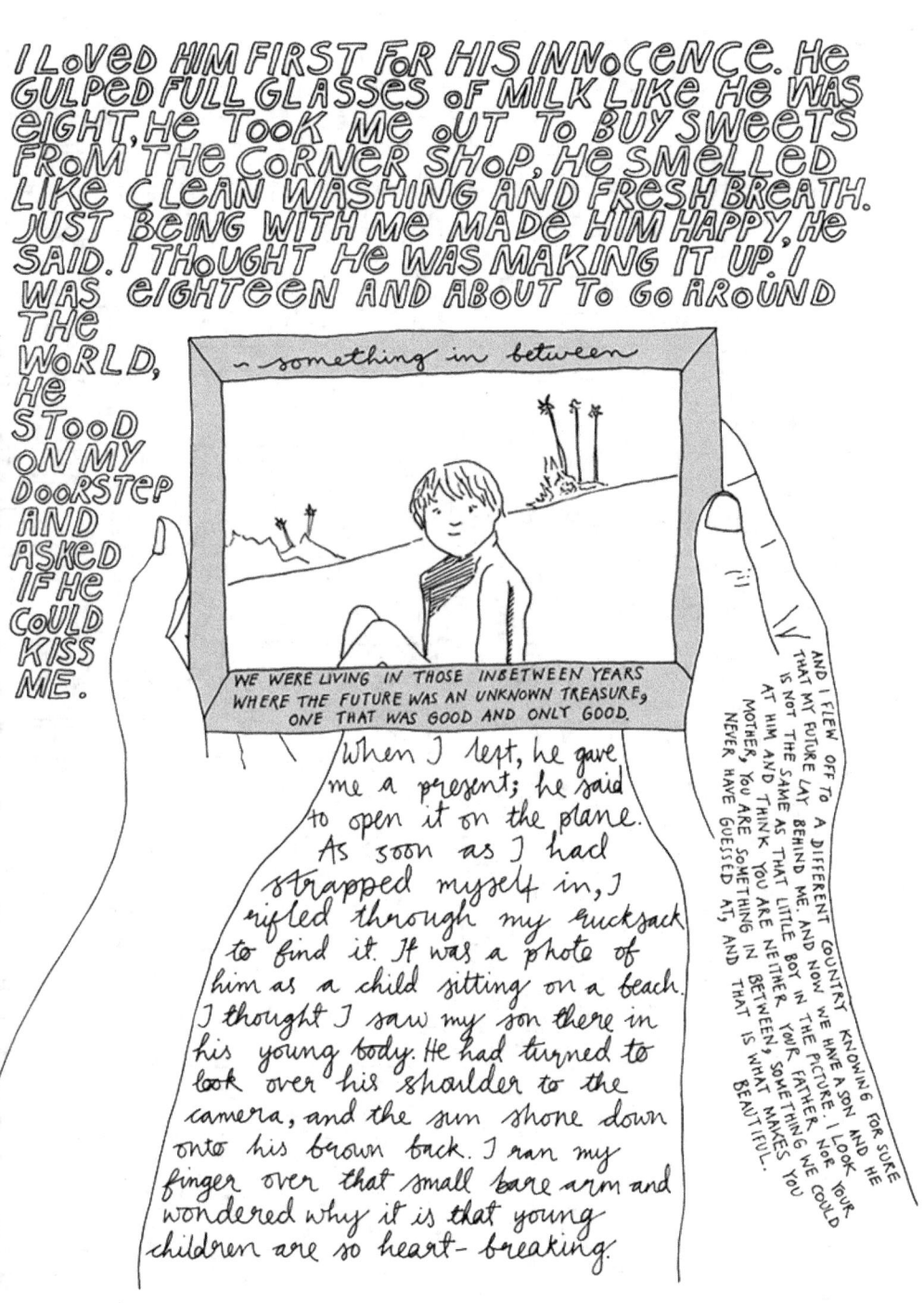

I LOVED HIM FIRST FOR HIS INNOCENCE. HE GULPED FULL GLASSES OF MILK LIKE HE WAS EIGHT, HE TOOK ME OUT TO BUY SWEETS FROM THE CORNER SHOP, HE SMELLED LIKE CLEAN WASHING AND FRESH BREATH. JUST BEING WITH ME MADE HIM HAPPY, HE SAID. I THOUGHT HE WAS MAKING IT UP. I WAS EIGHTEEN AND ABOUT TO GO AROUND THE WORLD, HE STOOD ON MY DOORSTEP AND ASKED IF HE COULD KISS ME.

— something in between

WE WERE LIVING IN THOSE INBETWEEN YEARS WHERE THE FUTURE WAS AN UNKNOWN TREASURE, ONE THAT WAS GOOD AND ONLY GOOD.

When I left, he gave me a present; he said to open it on the plane. As soon as I had strapped myself in, I rifled through my rucksack to find it. It was a photo of him as a child sitting on a beach. I thought I saw my son there in his young body. He had turned to look over his shoulder to the camera, and the sun shone down onto his brown back. I ran my finger over that small bare arm and wondered why it is that young children are so heart-breaking.

And I flew off to a different country knowing for sure that my future lay behind me. And now we have a son and he is not the same as that little boy in the picture. I look at him and think you are neither your father nor your mother, you are something in between, something we could never have guessed at, and that is what makes you beautiful.

Pied Piper

Walking down the high street,
where the cobbles send my boy to sleep
in his pushchair,
there is a woman playing the hang drum
she sits cross-legged on the pavement;
her clothes; layered, tatty,
her dreads scraped back into a hair band.
She looks down as she plays.

She curves around the drum and her
fingers play lightly like raindrops,
falling and running.
There are ten instruments at once coming from
the dome of this drum, bronze
and dimpled, held in the circle
of her body.
I walk on, and the notes follow me
like clear perfume down
this high street, that is
all shops and business
until this lightness comes.
It runs after me and I am one of the
Pied Piper's children, mesmerised,
enchanted.
I turn my head to
catch the last strains
of it, as it fades out of hearing.

A walk near Shere

'Big, big muddy puddles!' Sam said, over and over and he jumped in them until his shoes were wet through. Hail fell around us and the sky had turned dark, but it felt good to be outside, even still.

Waiting for you,
I could not explain the frustration
or the melancholy,
because I knew that you were safe,
the best kind of safe,
and that you would come
when you were ready.
But it felt like a sorrow in me,
something that was wrong,
something that I couldn't fix.
I missed you, I wanted to know you,
to touch your face, to hold you.
And now here you are, happily feeding,
your cool hands grasping at my skin,
your wrists no more than two centimetres wide.
You won't sleep on your own,
only between us, or on Daddy's chest,
so the nights are whispers, cuddles and half-light
and we don't mind at all.

LEMON CAKE

And the night after the frustrations, there is a clarity, like the first bite of a lemon cake or a gin and tonic, slipped down the neck. There is space for the first time in a long time. I am hair-washed, sitting in a house clean and dusted, the stillness of an orange dusk glowing outside. Ivy sleeps by me in the kitchen, in the night time light. It is so quiet that all I can hear is the click of the timer on the boiler, the little husky breaths she takes, the rattle of the cat flap as the cat runs in. There is nothing else, just the darkness of the window in front of me where I imagine people might be looking in, but I have become used to it, over time, this house, this little life.

moment

a moment to myself
while they sleep upstairs
conversations from the street outside
float through the window
a plane drones in the sky
I listen to the brush of sandpaper
on a window frame
the slam of a car door
the call of an unknown bird
It is these little things
      that I forget to listen for these days
above the delightful clamour of two small voices

crying in public places

This time it is me again, in a room of friends, a room of strangers. At the door of my son's preschool when he shouts 'don't like preschool' the whole way there, and leaps from the buggy board and runs off down the road. I hand him over, howling and have to turn from him and walk out of the door. Or he is as good as gold the whole morning, and holds it together until he stands there, coat off, ready for the day. And then he turns to me and quietly starts to cry, burying his face in my knee.

My boy, how could I describe him if you had not met him? He is a deer with his shining blue eyes, he is fierce and peaceful in a breath. I went up to do his stories tonight and he said 'go sleep mummy' and held my hand, and slipped off into his dreams, my lion-heart, dove gentle boy. And my girl, how would you know if you had not seen the curl of her eyelashes, the silky warmth of her cheek, the explosion of her laugh? We are shocked and in love with her, this faithful warrior, bursting with life and passion from every seam of herself.

I am happier now, than I have ever been. Two babies is what I was made for.

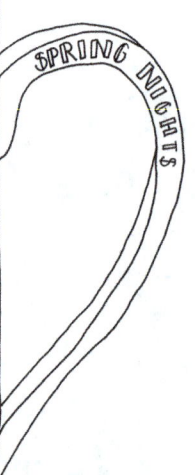

It was on those light, spring nights, in that tiny terrace, that they danced. They would strip to nothing after tea; peeling off their t-shirts with caked-on mash and beans, and twirl around. We never knew what to do with them for that hour after we had eaten, so we would leave the washing up and make hot tea, crash onto the sofa and watch as they span; these pearls of light, these wonders that had turned up in our lives, and consumed us so utterly. There was wonder in their eyes as they tried to get their bodies to move how they wanted, to get this thing called music under their skin.

december

the Fairy lights are on and twinkling, the children sleep in their bedroom. How wonderful, how mundane.

Yet there is someone who doesn't know; who can't feel the bite of this winter's air on her cheek, who cannot hear the blandness of her children's arguments and wish that they were in bed. She cannot feel the relief of handed in assignments, or know the crunch of a piece of toast smothered in jam.

I think of you Jo, all the time. Sad that you had to go so quickly. Angry, still, that you couldn't say goodbye.

And what have I loved the most, this weekend? Walking out of the wedding speeches to see lovely Charterhouse at dusk, where the children ran and ran across the cricket green, their feet bare upon the wet lawn, where the rain fell like mist on our cheeks and smudged the last of the light away.

AND THEN TODAY, ON THE BLOWY BEACH, WITH THE BLUE-GREY CLOUDS ON THE HORIZON, WE BURIED SAM UP TO HIS NECK IN THE SAND. THERE WAS THE SPACE, YOU SEE, TO BE QUIET AND TO RUN AND RUN,

AND THAT IS WHAT WE MOST NEEDED.

little park

"Can we go to the little park?" they'd say, and we'd make sweet tea and go over there.

It was quiet in the faded evenings, all the other children in their homes, watching TV. It was just us then, and our cat meowing through the fence.

It was my help. It was the first place we took to sunbathe his three day old son, through the four years living there, PACKED TIGHT AS SARDINES IN THAT TINY TERRACE.

The place where our tree grew, just for us, we said; It filled the window of our lounge with its shimmering, turning leaves.

SAMUEL LEARNT TO RIDE HIS YELLOW BIKE ANYTHING BUT WAIT BECAUSE THERE WAS A HOUSE SALE TO GO THROUGH AND ANOTHER BABY COMING

and we were standing there in the sun when we got the call to say that we'd got the house, - this mysterious 3 Church Road where we live now.

It's funny, the way things go, the moment things change, how we walk blind into blessings.

TREMBLING HEART

I HELD YOU TO ME ON THE BED AND SMELT YOUR HAIR, FELT YOUR LIGHTNESS, AS YOUR

FATHER BUSTLED IN THE DARKNESS FOR YOUR FAVOURITE THINGS.

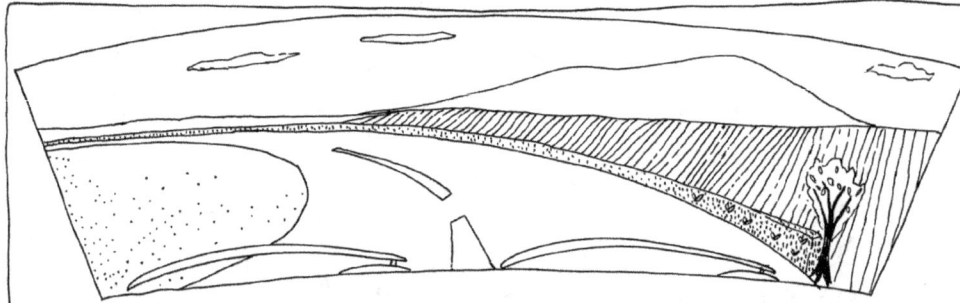

WE HAD BEEN TO THE DOCTORS THAT AFTERNOON AND HE RANG AS WE WERE DRIVING HOME TO THE CLEAR LIGHT, WHERE THE TOWN STOPPED AND THE HILLS BEGAN.

I SAW THE NUMBER FLASH UP ON THE SCREEN AND THOUGHT 'SHIT, IT'S SERIOUS.'

BUT I WASN'T PREPARED TO LISTEN TO THAT, WASN'T READY TO HAVE YOU HERE LIKE THIS, BREATHING AGAINST ME LIKE A BABY BIRD.

SOMETHING FAR DOWN IN ME HAD SENSED THAT IT WASN'T GOING TO GO AWAY,

YOUR FATHER HAD BROUGHT YOU HOME FROM THE HOSPITAL, IT WAS LATE AT NIGHT AND HE HAD TO TAKE YOU BACK AGAIN. HIS FACE WAS WHITE, AND HE WASN'T THINKING STRAIGHT. AND I HELD YOU ON THE BED THINKING THIS IS THE LAST TIME; THE LAST TIME THAT YOU ARE MINE, THAT YOU DO NOT HAVE DIABETES, THAT EVERYTHING IS OKAY.

I HAD TO KISS YOU GOODBYE AND SEND YOU OFF TO THAT WHITE, UNFORGIVING HOSPITAL WHILE I STAYED HOME FOR THE BABY,

BUT I REMEMBER HOLDING YOU ON THAT BED. THE DRUM OF MY HEART WAS LOUD, AND I WAS SO SMALL IN YOUR ARMS, AND ALL I HAD LEFT WAS THIS HELPLESSNESS.

type one

Walking out of hospital
on a cold but bright day,
clutching armfuls of her silly things;
Mr Carrot and Mr Strawberry.
her walking ahead of us
all jolly and bright,
singing even
in the October dusk,
and us following behind,
tearful and uncertain.
the bag of drugs they give us
to take home is almost as big as she is
and I feel more scared than I did
when our first-born came home,
swaddled with blankets and worry,
as the silver Sharan carried him.

thunderstorm

We are woken this morning by a rumble of thunder. You sit up in our bed at 5am and say 'I'M NOT SCARED OF THUNDERSTORMS ANYMORE' as if it is a perfectly reasonable thing to say at such a time. Later, there is a break in the rain and we walk through the farmer's field behind our house. The sky is big and beautiful, it stops me in my tracks and reminds me of my smallness; a good thing to remember sometimes.

It is half past nine when we step outside into our clear, beautiful garden and inhale a lungful each of this sweet night air. I pull the washing (still damp) from the line and you gather up the faded plastic toys that the kids have scattered around. We fold up the teepee, look up at the pink sky and think this life is good.

THE BELLS

YOU SHOULD HAVE SEEN IT TODAY, a thousand raindrops battering on the tarmac, shivering the leaves of the trees, drumming their green skin harder and faster. I held my Benjamin at the open window, HIS EYES LIT WITH WONDER. you should have heard it tonight, here in our front room, the clatter and DIN of the church bells so loud that they seemed to be shouting into the evening sky, "don't go to bed! joy, joy, joy!"

there are times like these where the sun is KIND in the morning, where it kisses your skin with sweetness, even your toes, still damp from the MORNING DEW. I remember it last year, my belly swelling under my clothes, the weight of my prayers on my shoulders, the sighs in my lungs each morning, but it was the KINDNESS of the sun that kept me going, as our feet wandered their way to the preschool.

Sometimes I want it to go on forever, the exhaustion that I feel this summer evening. There is an ache in my belly for these little people who need me. The thought of them growing up is too painful to think about just now, So let's pretend that you will always come and sit on my lap for cuddles, give me a kiss on the lips, hold my hand as we walk down the street.

LITTLE CAR

SHE WHISPERS TO ME IN HER BED,
        IN THE HALF-LIGHT.
SHE SAYS
  'there's a little car at Grandma's,
I'll show you, I'll get it out of the shed.'
SHE IS SERIOUS, HER FACE SET,
        HER EYES SHINING.
I CAN'T REMEMBER WHY SHE STARTED
  TALKING ABOUT THE CAR,
OR WHAT IT HAS TO DO WITH THE
    BOOK THAT WE WERE READING,

      BUT IT DOESN'T MATTER.
SHE IS *precious,*
      AND ALL OF HER
  THOUGHT TRAILS
     AND
     EACH
     OF HER BREATHS.

It is the moments like this that make it all worthwhile. The FIVE-THIRTY WAKE UP, AND THEN YOU COME OUTSIDE, LIKE THIS, AND YOU SEE THE BLUE GREY MIST WRAPPING AROUND THE MOUNTAINS, AND YOU SEE THE LIGHT OF DAWN COME BLAZING THROUGH, LIKE PURE GOLD. And even though you have hardly slept, here is a moment of life, of heaven touching earth. AND IT IS MADE EVEN MORE BEAUTIFUL, PERHAPS, BECAUSE OF HOW FRAGILE YOU FEEL, HOW TIRED. And it is a reminder that there is not just you, and your smallness and your lack, but there is something more.

The Sand martins dip and dive towards home, where their young await them, (heads peeping.) Across the river, we sit with our young tribe and think how fast the time has gone, and how they have grown; these three beauties that we are in some way and in no way responsible for. We sit quietly, watching as the brook runs on.

Uncoupling

two metal fists
u n c l e n c h
and the one truck slips
silently
back
into the inky night.

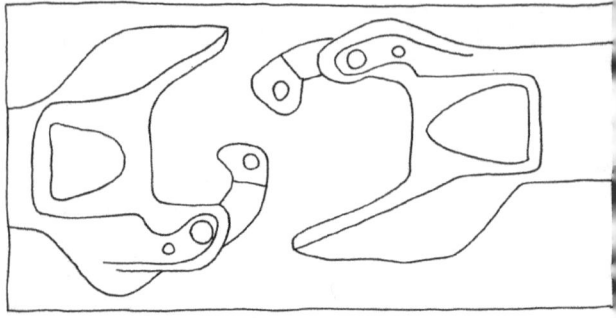

there is a stunned silence between us,

we were not waiting for this. How could we have counted the cost when we did not see this coming?

We thought that we would see home again,

that things would go back to how they were before, but they have not, and never will,

and we know that now.

There are secret losses, perhaps, borne

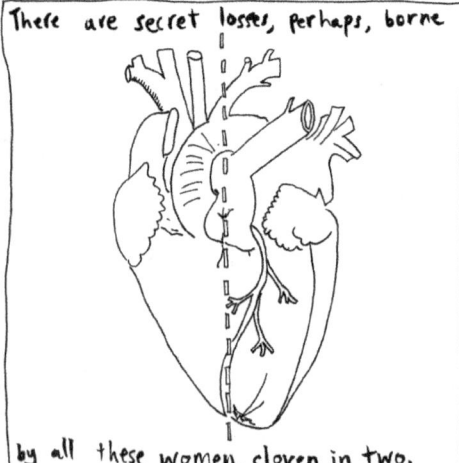

by all these women, cloven in two,

borne by all these men who are unchanged,

but for whom the world has changed.

We used to give up anything for our love, it was well-fed and watered,

but now we say there is not the time. It never seems there is enough; and I think of that truck **slipping silently back,** of the men on the tracks who didn't even hear it coming; it took them clean away.

We thought they would come up like bubbles, these children, finding the light innately, by their very beings, so full of fire and oxygen.

Before, on that other shore, that I can't remember now, there seemed a lack, a missingness that I was desperate to fill,

but it has become an open wound of terrible love, one that will never heal, not now,

and things will never be as they were, for our hearts are walking around outside of us; we are no longer ourselves,

and this is why I think of those trucks, uncoupling, as I lie next to you, in the black night, our daughter next to me on the bed, our son crying out in the other room.

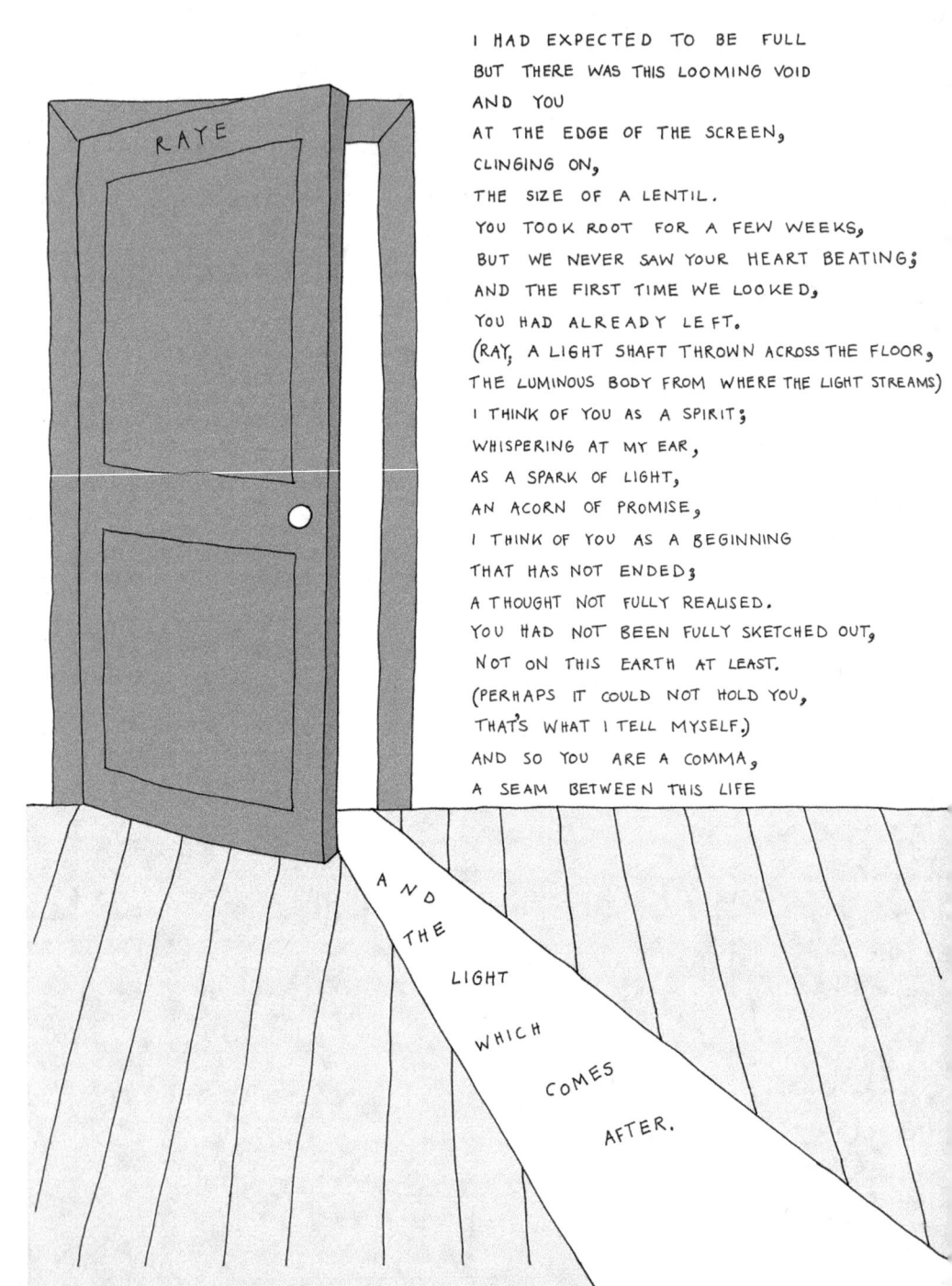

About the Author

Elisabeth lives in Shropshire with her husband and three children. She teaches creative writing, creates her own hand-lettered poems and takes commissions. She also writes short stories, fiction and poetry. Her work has been published in Third Way, The Guardian, Fractured West, and at xenith.net amongst others. She has previously worked as a bookseller and librarian and holds a masters in creative writing from Goldsmiths University, London. She likes cities, long train journeys and old photographs.

Find her at:

etsy.com/uk/shop/LittleBirdEditions

elisabethpike.co.uk

All poems Copyright Elisabeth Pike 2017.

www.ingramcontent.com/pod-product-compliance
Lightning Source LLC
Chambersburg PA
CBHW052207070526
44585CB00017B/2108